I0159585

Get Ready, Aim, Shoot
Hit Your Bull's Eye this Year

A Spiritual Guide to
Using the Secular or Jewish
New Year to Reset Your
Personal, Professional and
Spiritual Targets

Nina Amir

Get Ready, Aim, Shoot: Hit Your Bull's eye this Year
Copyright © 2011 by Nina Amir. All rights reserved.

All rights reserved. No part of this book may be reproduced or transmitted in any form or by any means, electronic or mechanical, including photocopying, recording or by an information storage and retrieval system, without written permission from the author.

ISBN 9780983535300

Printed in the United States of America by 360DigitalBooks.com (www.360digitalbooks.com).

Published by:

Pure Spirit Creations
15383 Stetson Road
Los Gatos, CA 95033
408-353-1943
www.purespiritcreations.com

Table of Contents

Table of Contents

Introduction

If you are reading this book, it's likely that either December 31st, the secular New Year, or Rosh Hashanah, the Jewish New Year, are fast approaching or have just passed. Both New Year's Eve and Rosh Hashanah mark the end of one year and the beginning of another, although each commemorates the old and brings in the new in a slightly different manner. Yet, each has one thing in common — a focus on developing New Year's resolutions or goals.

These goals may be personal, professional or spiritual. They may involve business and career, health and well being, relationship and romance, prayer and ritual. No matter what goals you set, the New Year marks a time of planning to turn over a new leaf, to start fresh, to do things better, to this time — maybe — actually follow through and achieve those goals.

In fact, only four out of five people who go to the trouble of setting New Year's goals ever achieve them. Interestingly, we call these New Year's "resolutions," but it seems few of us really resolve to accomplish them.

Stop for a moment and think about the word "resolve." For most of us it holds a negative connotation. It isn't that we want to make the change. We are resolved that we must. We've made the decision and are determined to follow through.

With that attitude, it's no wonder we don't change or achieve our goals. If we aren't passionate about the goals we set, if we aren't committed at a deep level to achieving them — and if we don't have the tools to actually accomplish them, we quickly go right back to our old ways or habits.

Whether or not you are Jewish, Judaism's manner of looking at the New Year and the goals we set at that time of the year, typically in the fall, provides a helpful guide for actually achieving these goals and creating lasting change in our lives. That's why this book focuses on the process used by most Jews during the Jewish New Year to "set new targets" and hit them.

If you are Jewish, you'll enjoy taking a deeper look at how your religion can help you create change in your life. If you follow another religion, or if you are not religious at all, this ancient wisdom and philosophy offers a powerful process you can still put to use in your life at any time of the year. Also, know that what is written in these pages is a distillation of the teachings of Judaism put through the lens of my own understanding. That understanding is distilled through my own studies of a variety of human potential techniques and tools as well. Therefore, what you read here goes beyond simple Judaism and becomes a self-improvement tool for all those wanting to make lasting changes in their lives.

In other words, don't be put off by the Jewish terminology or teachings. Simply look for the wisdom, the tools, the principles, or the exercises that feel right and useful to you. Then put them to work in your life this year. In fact, put them to use right now. You'll be amazed at the results you achieve.

The *Real* Sin: Not Setting Targets and Trying to Hit the Mark

Most people don't realize that by its choice of words, the Old Testament places emphasis on goal setting. In fact, it seems that God expects us to set targets for ourselves and at least to try to hit them.

No matter our religious orientation — or lack thereof, we can all learn something from the use of the world "sin" in the Old Testament and in Jewish liturgy. Let me explain why. The word for sin in Hebrew — *chet* — comes from the sport of archery. Hebrew has no real word for sin as we understand it. One or two other words refer to what we think of as sin, but no one word actually means "sin" per se. The words *al chet*, usually translated as "the sin" and commonly used during the Jewish High Holy Days (the Jewish New Year, *Rosh Hashanah*, and the Day of Repentance, *Yom Kippur*) really mean "the missed mark." In archery terms, this would refer to missing the target or not hitting the bull's eye. Interestingly, the word Torah, which refers to the Old Testament scrolls and the text they contain (the Five Books of Moses), also comes from archery. It means to take aim. Thus, the Old Testament teaches us to take aim, but sometimes we take aim and miss the mark, which in Judaism — and during biblical times — is considered a serious enough offense to be called a "sin."

Why do the Old Testament, Hebrew and Judaism use archery terminology for such important words as sin and Torah? And why are these words associated with taking aim and hitting or missing targets? After all, sins are not something to be taken lightly, and the Torah is the sacred text of Judaism. The reason lies in the analogy between an archer missing his mark and a person repenting for wrongs committed.

Archery involves setting up targets in the middle of which are the bull's eyes at which the archer aims his arrows. To hit the mark, archers must practice their aim until they become good enough to hit not only the target but the bull's eye. Between the Jewish New Year, Rosh Hashanah, and the Day of Repentance, Yom Kippur, Jews look at the past 12 months of their lives to see what targets they set up for themselves, how they practiced hitting that target and if their aim was true. They look at the target to see if they managed to hit the bull's eye. During this period of introspection they notice not only if they aimed their arrows and shot, but if they even got close to their mark. If not, the period between the two holidays provides a time to set up new targets — or to reexamine or study old targets — and to commit to practicing their aim. It's also a time to set the intention — *kavanah* (another word that, while not related to archery, also means "to aim") — to try harder to shoot true, to hit the bull's eye this year. Finally, this period offers a chance to ask for forgiveness for missing the mark — for not aiming, for not shooting, for not practicing, for not hitting the mark — during the last year. Jews ask forgiveness of others, of themselves and of God.

If we look at this Jewish New Year's practice — a practice that comes out of the Jewish tradition but is relevant for anyone from any religious background — we see clearly why archery terms are used to describe sin. God appears to be telling us that the sin comes in not setting goals for ourselves and in not trying to achieve them. At a minimum we have to set up a target, try to take aim, practice shooting that arrow, and then let it fly. We have to attempt to hit our mark. The sin lies not in simply missing the mark but in not trying to hit it at all. If we can sincerely say we tried to hit the target — we aimed, we practiced shooting, we shot, and we still didn't get a bull's eye, God forgives us.

The importance of actually setting New Year's resolutions or goals can be found in the answer to this question: What would happen if we never set a target for ourselves, if we never had any goals, aspirations or resolutions? We would never change. We would never move forward. We would never grow. We would never achieve or accomplish anything. We would not fulfill our potential or live our lives fully. That truly constitutes a sin.

Our goals and resolutions give us something to move towards — something quantifiable. The secular or Jewish New Year provides the perfect time to turn over a new leaf, begin again, think about what we want to change or accomplish, how we want to grow, to set up those new targets so we can reach our full potential and live our lives fully.

Exercise:

Evaluate Your Aim Last Year

What targets — goals or resolutions — did you set last year at this time? List them here.

Did you hit or miss your mark during the course of the year? In other words, did you achieve your goals or keep your resolutions? Did you make the changes you wanted to make, move toward your dreams and desires, make any progress towards accomplishing what you set out to do? For each goal or resolution you mentioned on the last page here on this page write down how much progress you made towards achieving or accomplishing it. Also explain why you feel you missed the mark. Now go back to the last page and in a colored pen or pencil write next to each target, "missed the mark," "hit the mark" or "came close to hitting the mark."

How to Improve Your Aim

How do we know what new targets we want to set? By taking the opportunity afforded us by the end of the year to measure whether or not we got close to our goal, whether we took baby steps or big giant steps towards following through with our resolutions, and whether our arrow hit near the outside of the target or right smack in the middle of the bull's eye. We can look back at how we missed — or hit — the mark and learn from this experience, thereby improving our aim, refocusing our targets and preparing to try again to hit the bull's eye in the coming year.

While Rosh Hashanah marks the joyous beginning of a new year, it also begins a somber period of introspection mentioned previously called the "Days of Awe," the period between the Jewish New Year and the end of Yom Kippur. During Rosh Hashanah, Jews begin the process of t'shuvah, a Hebrew word meaning repentance which comes from the root "to turn or to return." They turn their attention away from outward denial of wrongdoing and toward acknowledgement of sins — the places where they missed the mark, away from unwanted behavior and toward their best self. They take an accounting of their behavior in all aspects of their life — personal, professional and spiritual, and they look not only at how to make amends for anything they might need to correct but at how to improve their behavior in the future. This includes, of course, setting new goals for the coming year. Since they are examining how they missed the mark, they must begin setting up new targets at which to aim.

Just before the secular New Year, or even just after, most people benefit by going through a process of introspection and of t'shuvah, of return to their best selves. We can examine our lives over the past 12 months carefully, honestly looking at how we can improve our actions, behaviors and habits. We can use what we learn about our past performance to structure our new goals, resolutions and targets. We can discern where our aim was off and where we needed some target practice. This helps us get closer to hitting the mark in the months to come.

Carlos Castaneda, author of *The Teachings of Don Juan*, wrote of living with death on your shoulder. While it's not so pleasant to live every day with the thought in your mind that you might die, it's not a bad idea once a year to look at your life from that perspective. The Jewish New Year liturgy speaks of people "being written in the Book of Life." This metaphor reminds us we are fragile and don't know whether we will survive the year or not. Should we not survive, we might want to re-evaluate our priorities. With this in mind, we rethink our goals for the year. What would we like to be doing? How might we like to be living? In what way do we want to spend our time? How can we live our life fully? What can we do to reach our fullest potential?

We don't often think of change as easy. It seems easier to stay the way we are and where we are. Yet, change is inevitable and often forced upon us. When the New Year rolls around, however, we aren't forced to change. We can choose to change. On Rosh Hashanah, Jews are asked to change, reminded of the necessity of change — change for the better. On the secular New Year, we can see resolutions as an obligation and resolve to change. Or we can see New Year's resolutions in the same light as the Jewish New Year — as an opportunity for change, as a chance to reset our targets, to correct our aim, and to try once again to hit the bull's eye. We can see the New Year as a chance to make our bull's eye one of fulfilling our own personal potential and living our life to the fullest extent possible.

Exercise:
Improve Your Aim and Set New Targets

To begin the process of t'shuvah, returning to your best self, answer the following questions. As you answer them, you will develop your focus — intention (kavanah) — for the coming year and improve your aim.

Look back over the past 12 months. How did you live, play, work, love, and behave? In general, describe what would you have changed about how you lived your life last year?

How could you have been a better you last year?

What would you like to do more of this year?

What would you like to do less of this year?

How can you live your life fully this year?

What can you do to reach your fullest potential this year?

Write down at least three new goals — targets you want to hit — for this New Year.

1.

2.

3.

For each goal, list three things you can do to help move you closer to achieving that goal. These might be specific actions you can take or habits you can form that will bring you closer to hitting that bull's eye or to accomplishing your goal.

1.

   a.

   b.

   c.

2.

   a.

   b.

   c.

3.

   a.

   b.

   c.

Write an intention statement to go with each of your goals. Make the statement quantifiable. For example, if your goal is to lose 10 pounds in the next 12 months you might write, "I intend to be fit, trim, and 10 pounds lighter by this time next year."

1.

2.

3.

How to Seal Your Fate

Jews are told that on the Jewish New Year "it is written" and on the Day of Repentance "it is sealed." What is "it"? Our fate for the next year. Where is it "written and sealed"? In the Book of Life.

So, is the Book of Life figurative or literal? Is it a poetic or a concrete use of words? Most say it is both figurative and poetic. Yet, just as God supposedly can seal our fate for the coming year, we possess the ability to do the same. We can "write" it by coming up with our targets — our goals and resolutions — and honing our aim and practicing our skill. Then, we can "seal" our fate both by taking action towards those goals and resolutions and also by visualizing ourselves having achieved our goal. We can see ourselves in our mind shooting that arrow and the arrow landing right in the middle of the bull's eye, and then we can go and actually do just that in the real world.

Many athletes use this technique to help them succeed in their sports. They see themselves running the race and crossing the finish line ahead of the other racers. They see themselves connecting the bat with the ball time after time. They see themselves performing their gymnastics routine to perfection. Then they see themselves standing on the podium receiving their gold medal or award.

If we can see ourselves having followed through on our resolution or having accomplished our goal — if we can see that arrow suspended from the bull's eye — then we will find it much easier to actually do so in real life. You see, the subconscious mind does not know the difference between what we visualize and what we actually do. So, when we visualize our resolutions achieved and our goals accomplished, it thinks we have done so already. In fact, as we visualize ourselves achieving those goals, for instance, shooting an arrow and hitting the target, the mind causes our muscles to react as if we were actually placing the arrow in the bow, pulling it back, and releasing it. Our eyes even respond as if we were watching it sail through the air and hit the target. If we can muster up the emotions that would go with seeing the arrow actually hit the bull's eye, our body will actually register those emotions as well. If we visualize this often enough, then when we actually shoot the arrow, our body has been conditioned to aim, shoot, and hit the target. We've mentally performed target practice. We've improved our aim and our ability to hit that bull's eye.

Then we must actually take action. We must do whatever we have visualized. Apply for a new job. Participate in the new exercise program. Heal the relationship with a spouse. Stop smoking or drinking. We must do what we visualize. We seal our fate.

How do we seal our goals for the New Year in the Book of Life? We write our goals down, visualize our goals in fine detail and feel exactly what it would be like if we had already manifested the results we desire. Then we take appropriate action to manifest those goals. Two simple steps: Imagine the life you want, the behaviors to which you aspire as if they were published in that book — sealed, already accomplished. Then go out into life and seal the book by living that life and those behaviors and by achieving those goals and dreams.

Exercise:
Write Yourself Into the Book of Life

Imagine a beautiful book, a quill pen and a jar of ink lying on a table before you. You open the book and find that it contains the story of your life up to this very moment. You turn the page and discover that tomorrow's entry and the next and the next are empty. The pages are a beautiful white, waiting for someone to write down the details of what you will do next, what will happen next. You pick up the quill, dip it in the ink and begin to write. Imagine not only the next moment, hour, day, but the next week, month and year.

On the next page, write down your vision of the next year in the Book of Life as if it is happening now. As you inscribe each word, feel as if you are experiencing all that you are writing — as if each event you describe is happening to you at this moment. As you finish your entry or entries, take another piece of paper and blot the ink as if you are sealing it.

Exercise:
Create a Visionary Description of Your Targets

Using the same three goals you chose in the earlier exercise, write a visionary description of what it would be like to have accomplished each of them. Write about them in the past tense, as if you had already accomplished your resolution, achieved your goal or hit the target. As you write, try to feel the emotions you would feel upon seeing your arrow in the middle of the bull's eye.

Exercise:
What Stops You from Hitting the Mark?

Sometimes we set goals or resolutions and despite our best intentions and efforts we don't achieve them. If we have followed through with our resolutions, if we have taken every possible step towards our goals, then we have to look inside again to see if something emotional or psychological is stopping us from hitting the mark.

If your goals or resolutions are similar this year to the ones you set last year because you missed the mark or didn't even shoot your arrow at the target, ask yourself the following questions.

Do you feel worthy of achieving your goal? If "yes," then why don't you do so? If "no," why don't you feel worthy and how does this lack of self-worth stop you from hitting your mark?

Do you feel good enough about yourself to accomplish what you desire? If "no," why not? If "yes," why then don't you hit your target?

Do you believe you are capable of following through on your resolutions or accomplishing your goals? If "no," why not? And what can you do to become capable? (Add these things to your goals.) If "yes," why don't you use your skills to hit your targets?

Are you afraid of your own success? If you answered "yes," Why? If "no," is there some other aspect of success that stops you from hitting your target?

What is your "payoff" for missing the mark? What do you gain by not achieving your goal or following through on your resolutions? What new positive payoff can you give yourself to help you begin taking aim, practicing your shot, and actually shooting at your target?

Knowing that taking action is necessary to achieving your goals, answer this question: What actions can you take to be sure you achieve your goals?

1.

2.

3.

4.

5.

What is one reason why this year you will not only set your targets but hit them?

(*Note:* After answering the questions in this section, you may want to go back and repeat some of the exercises.)

Conclusion

Although this book was written for use on the Jewish or secular New Year, you can use its principles, tools and practices at any point during the year when you feel the need to evaluate your progress towards your goals and resolutions. Just like an archer who approaches the target to look at where the arrows have landed and then remove them before returning to the shooting line to begin target practice again, you must sometimes stop and see if your aim has been true, refocus, true up your aim, and begin shooting again. It's always helpful to take a little time for introspection, to do t'shuvah — turn back to your best self, remember your kavanah — intention, or to reset your targets based on what you learn.

Keep this book handy all year long. Use the process within its pages any time you want to reset your personal, professional or spiritual targets, and then get ready, aim, shoot and hit your bull's eye.

About the Author

Nina Amir, Your Inspiration-to-Creation Coach, inspires people to create the results they desire. When working with writers, she inspires them to create publishable and published products and careers as writers and authors. She inspires people to create fully-lived lives; cherished dreams, desires and goals; and meaning-full and spirit-full rituals and practices. In all cases, she challenges them to find and fulfill their purpose and realize their potential.

Nina is a seasoned journalist, editor, writing and author coach; *maggid* (Jewish inspirational speaker); Kabbalistic conscious creation coach; and the regular holiday and spirituality expert on *Conversations with Mrs. Claus*, a weekly podcast heard in more than 90 countries and downloaded by 130,000 listeners per month. She holds a BA in magazine journalism from Syracuse University's S.I Newhouse School of Public Communication with a concentration in psychology, is a life coach, a certified rebirther, and is trained as a Tarot reader and as a Voice Dialogue facilitator.

Through her writing and speaking, Nina offers human potential, personal growth, self-improvement, and practical spiritual tools. Although she often speaks and writes from a Jewish perspective, her work spans religious lines and is pertinent to people of all faiths and spiritual traditions. She also is a popular writer, blogger and speaker on topics related to publishing and writing. In all she does, Nina focuses on helping people live their lives fully and manifest their desires — whether those desires look like written products or something entirely different.

Nina sees herself as an "Everywoman" whose struggles and successes are not unlike anyone else's. Therefore, she writes, speaks and teaches from a place of knowing that what has worked for her will at least provide others with a starting place from which to find what works best for them.

She lives in the Santa Cruz Mountains above Los Gatos, CA, with her husband and two children.

Other Products from
Pure Spirit Creations

The Kabbalah of Conscious Creation
How to Mystically Manifest
Your Physical and Spiritual Desires

This booklet takes you through the four Kabbalistic worlds of creation to help you manifest your desires while also teaching you how to become not only a receiver but a giver as well, thereby developing a connection with the Ultimate Creator and tapping into the Divine flow of giving and receiving. Designed with short, easy-to-understand chapters, this booklet includes tips, tools and meditations for creating what you want and need on the physical and spiritual planes.

Travel through the four Kabbalistic "worlds" of creation:

- **Being** — where inspiration and desire are born
- **Thinking** — where desires are formed into thoughts and words
- **Feeling** — where thoughts are combined with feelings of manifested desires
- **Doing** — where inspired action moves us to complete the act of creation

This is the Law of Attraction through a Jewish mystical lens—but it is applicable to anyone from any religious background or spiritual tradition.

Navigating the Narrow Bridge
7 Steps for
Moving Forward Courageously
Even When Life Seems Most Precarious

Are you one of the 6.3 million Americans who have some specific fear? If you feel immobilized by fear, this short book offers tools for moving freely, confidently and joyously through life and towards your goals and desires. Discover seven steps to help you get from where you are to where you want to be despite your fear. Learn to live with faith, courage and the joy that comes from see the miracle of life itself.

No matter how much or how little fear you feel – or for what reason, that fear stops you from living your life fully and creating the life you desire. Fear prevents you from achieving your highest potential and paralyzes you on the path to your dreams.

Learn to move through your fear so you can achieve your highest potential and achieve your dreams. According to Rebbe Nachman, who lived from 1772-1840, we need to know one thing: "A person walks in life on a narrow bridge. The most important thing is not to make ourselves afraid."

Navigating the Narrow Bridge draws on the teachings of Rebbe Nachman, metaphysical and quantum physics principles, spiritual wisdom, and human potential techniques. Thus, it is pertinent to anyone from any religious or spiritual background or tradition. Indeed, it's appropriate for anyone who simply wants to walk courageously through life.

The Priestess Practice
4 Steps to Creating Sacred Space an
Inviting the Divine to Dwell Within It

In the ancient Temple in Jerusalem, the *kohenim*, or priests, used to prepare the sacred space, light the candles and invoke the Divine Presence. With no priests and no temple, today these duties fall to modern-day priestesses — *kohanot*. Each Friday night Jewish women all over the world prepare their homes for the Sabbath, light the Shabbat candles and say the blessing that invites the *Shechinah*, the Divine Feminine, into their homes. As they do, they symbolically act out the role of the Temple priests and become priestesses.

Realize your dream of becoming a priestess. Take on Shabbat candle lighting as a spiritual practice. Preside as a *kohenet*, a priestess, over the sacred space you create and the ritual you perform. Invite the Divine Feminine Presence into your sanctuary and then dwell there with Her.

This 34-page booklet provides the perfect guide for those wanting to draw out their Inner Priestess. In addition to its four clearly-described steps, the booklet offers three easily-used tools for awakening your Inner Priestess, officiating over both the beginning and end of the Sabbath and visualizing yourself anointed as a kohenet.

10 Days & 10 Ways to Return to Your Best Self
A Human Potential Tool
Bridging Religious Traditions

Would you like to have a process that helps you return to your best self — and to Source — in just 10 awesome days? The 10-day period known as the Days of Awe provide a time for anyone, not just Jews, to go inward and to consider how to "do *t'shuvah*," to turn back to God and to their soul. You can use this time to consider not only your sins and how to rectify them but how to achieve your full human potential.

This book provides 10-days of exercises to help you go through an introspective process for the period between Rosh Hashanah, the Jewish New Year, and Yom Kippur, the Day of Repentance. However, the book is appropriate for use by anyone at any time of the year.

For more information on Nina Amir,
her products and services, or to book a
speaking engagement, please visit:

www.purespiritcreations.com
or
www.ninaamir.com

Or contact Nina Amir at:

Pure Spirit Creations
15383 Stetson Road
Los Gatos, CA 95033
408-353-1943
Namir@purespiritcreations.com

www.ingramcontent.com/pod-product-compliance
Lightning Source LLC
Chambersburg PA
CBHW060634030426
42337CB00018B/3357

* 9 7 8 0 9 8 3 5 3 5 3 0 0 *